CABLE
ready ™

Edited by Kara Gott Warner

HOUSE of
WHITE
BIRCHES

PUBLISHERS
SINCE 1947

Introduction

Cablework knitting creates visual interest and dimension to any design. Cables are easy to master, and they add the look of complexity to even the simplest of projects. In this book you'll find 10 fashionable designs consisting of cardigans, shrugs, scarves and cowls. And if you're short on time, you'll find an assortment of quick-to-knit cowls that you could make in just one weekend.

If you're new to cable knitting, or if you're looking for a quick refresher, our comprehensive tutorial shows you step-by-step how to work a basic 2 x 2 cable. This instructional guide also provides an example of a cable chart so you can better understand what standard cable symbols look like and how to read them. These principles can be applied to any cable once the process is mastered.

Let's explore the many twists and turns that cable knitting has to offer!

Kara

Kara Gott Warner, editor

Table of Contents

Diamond Cabled Cardi, page 19

Bobbles Beyond Compare, page 31

Magic Cable Cardigan, page 9

How to Knit Cables in Three Easy Steps

Cables are much easier to knit than they appear. There are just three easy steps for working a basic cable.

Step 1: Slide stitches onto a cable needle to hold them out of the way temporarily.

Step 2: Work the next stitches on the left-hand needle.

Step 3: Work the stitches from the cable needle.

The pattern will always be specific as to how many stitches to slide onto the cable needle. It also will tell you whether the cable needle is to be held in front or in back of the work. This is very important because this is what causes the cable to twist to the left or to the right. Charts make it easy to see what the cable should look like—the chart symbols look like an actual cable. Charts always have an explanation for what each symbol means.

Try this basic 2/2 cable in a swatch that can also function as your gauge swatch for the Easiest Cable Shrug, a perfect beginner cable knitter's project. It is called a 2/2 cable because 2 stitches cross over 2 stitches. The same steps are used when 3 stitches cross over 3 stitches or any number described in the instructions. 2/2 LC indicates that cable will cross to the left, so the stitches on the cable needle are held to the front. 2/2 RC indicates that the cable will cross to the right, so the stitches on the cable needle are held to the back.

You will need knitting needles and a cable needle. Cable needles vary in length and shape so experiment with different styles to find one that you like. Always use a cable needle that is smaller in diameter when compared to your knitting needles.

2 over 2 Left-Cross Cable

Rows 1 and 3 (RS): [P1, k1] 6 times, p2, k4, p2, [k1, p1] 6 times.

Rows 2 and 4 (WS): [K1, p1] 5 times, p2, k2, p4, k2, p2, [k1, p1] 5 times.

Row 5: [P1, k1] 6 times, p2, 2/2 LC, p2, [k1, p1] 6 times.

Row 6: Rep Row 2.

Cast on 32 sts. Work Rows 1–4, then work Row 5 until you get to 2/2 LC.

To work the 2/2 LC:

Step 1: Slip 2 stitches onto the cable needle purlwise so they don't twist. Position the cable needle in front of your work.

Step 1 (2/2 LC)

Step 2: Knit the next 2 stitches from the left needle. Knit the stitches firmly so that the stitches don't get loose from being stretched.

Step 2 (2/2 LC)

Step 3: Knit the 2 stitches from the cable needle, again tugging them snug just a bit. Continue in pattern across the row.

Step 3 (2/2 LC)

Finish with Row 6 of the pattern.

The 2nd version is very similar, with only the cable turn being worked differently. The cable-turn abbreviation is 2/2 RC, which means that 2 stitches are crossing to the right over 2 stitches.

2 over 2 Right-Cross Cable

Rows 1 and 3 (RS): [P1, k1] 6 times, p2, k4, p2, [k1, p1] 6 times.

Rows 2 and 4 (WS): [K1, p1] 5 times, p2, k2, p4, k2, p2, [k1, p1] 5 times.

Row 5: [P1, k1] 6 times, p2, 2/2RC, p2, [k1, p1] 6 times.

Row 6: Rep Row 2.

Cast on 32 sts. Work Rows 1–4, then work Row 5 until you get to the 2/2 RC.

To work the 2/2 RC:

Step 1: Slip 2 stitches onto the cable needle purlwise so they don't twist. Position the cable needle in back of your work.

Step 1 (2/2 RC)

Step 2: Knit the next 2 stitches from the left-hand needle. Knit the stitches firmly so that the stitches don't get loose from being stretched.

Step 2 (2/2 RC)

Step 3: Knit the 2 stitches from the cable needle, again tugging them snug just a bit. Continue in pattern across the row.

Step 3 (2/2 RC)

Finish with Row 6 of the pattern. •

STITCH KEY
☐ K on RS, p on WS
▬ P on RS, k on WS
⧓ 2/2 RC
⧓ 2/2 LC

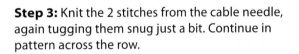

SWATCH 2 WITH 2/2 LC

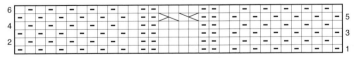

SWATCH 1 WITH 2/2 RC

Easiest Cable Shrug

Although cables look complicated, they are actually very simple. The shape of this shrug is a basic rectangle so there is no shaping to distract you from focusing on your knitting.

Design by Lorna Miser

Skill Level
■■■□ INTERMEDIATE

Sizes
Woman's small (medium, large, extra-large, 2X-large) Instructions are given for smallest size, with larger sizes in parentheses. When only 1 number is given, it applies to all sizes.

Finished Measurements
Width: 28 (31, 33, 36, 38) inches
Length: 24 (26, 28, 30, 32) inches

Materials
- Universal Yarn Blossom Street Collection Cashmere Fleur De Lys (worsted weight; 90% extra-fine merino wool/10% cashmere; 93 yds/50g per ball): 7 (8, 9, 10, 11) balls valour #408
- Size 8 (5mm) needles or size needed to obtain gauge
- Cable needle

4 MEDIUM

Gauge
19 sts and 25 rows = 4 inches/10cm in seed st.

To save time, take time to check gauge.

Special Abbreviation
2 over 2 Left Cross (2/2 LC): Sl 2 to cn and hold in front, k2, k2 from cn.

Pattern Stitches
K2, P2 Rib (multiple of 4 sts + 2)
Row 1 (RS): K2, *p2, k2; rep from * across.
Row 2: P2, *k2, p2; rep from * across.
Rep Rows 1 and 2 for pat.

Seed Stitch (even number)
Row 1: *K1, p1; rep from * across.
Rep Row 1 for pat.

Cable Panel (10-st panel)
Rows 1 and 5 (RS): K1, p2, k4, p2, k1.
Row 2 and all WS rows: P1, k2, p4, k2, p1.
Row 3: K1, p2, 2/2 LC, p2, k1.
Row 6: Rep Row 2.
Rep Rows 1–6 for pat.

Pattern Notes

The shrug is worked as a rectangle and, once seamed, has no top or bottom and can be worn either way; one ribbed edging will fold to form a collar at the neck edge.

Shrug

Cast on 134 (146, 158, 170, 182) sts.

Work 4 inches in K2, P2 Rib, ending with a WS row.

Set-up row (RS): Work 14 (16, 18, 20, 22) sts in seed st, *work Cable Panel across 10 sts, work 14 (16, 18, 20, 22) sts in seed st; rep from * 4 more times.

Work even in established pats until shrug measures 20 (22, 24, 26, 28) inches.

Work 4 inches in K2, P2 Rib.

Bind off loosely in rib.

Finishing

Weave in ends. Block to finished measurements.

Fold shrug in half horizontally holding cast-on and bound-off edges together.

Sew side seams, leaving 7 inches open for armholes. ●

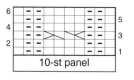

10-st panel

CABLE PANEL

STITCH KEY

☐	K on RS, p on WS
–	P on RS, k on WS
⧖	2/2 LC

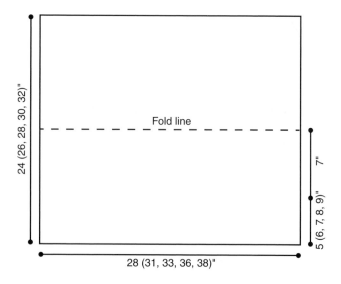

Fold line

24 (26, 28, 30, 32)"

7"

5 (6, 7, 8, 9)"

28 (31, 33, 36, 38)"

Magic Cable Cardigan

Wear this unique piece with the cables draping your torso. Or, flip it around to allow the ribbing to surround your neck. Either way you can't go wrong.

Design by Lorna Miser

Skill Level
■■■□ INTERMEDIATE

Sizes
Woman's small (medium, large, extra-large, 2X-large) Instructions are given for smallest size, with larger sizes in parentheses. When only 1 number is given, it applies to all sizes.

Finished Measurements
Width from cuff to cuff: 60 (60, 60, 60, 62) inches
Length: 21 (21½, 24, 24½, 27) inches

Materials
- Mirasol Sulka (heavy worsted weight; 60% merino wool/ 20% alpaca/20% silk; 55 yds/50g per skein): 16 (18, 20, 21, 24) skeins raspberry #215
- Size 10 (6mm) straight and 24-inch circular needles or size needed to obtain gauge
- Spare circular needle
- Size J/10 (6mm) crochet hook
- Cable needle

Gauge
15 sts and 17 rows = 4 inches/10cm in St st.

To save time, take time to check gauge.

Special Abbreviation
2 over 2 Right Cross (2/2 RC): Sl 2 to cn and hold in back, k2, k2 from cn.

Pattern Stitches
K2, P2 Rib (multiple of 4 sts + 2)
Row 1 (RS): K2, *p2, k2; rep from * across.
Row 2: P2, *k2, p2; rep from * across.
Rep Rows 1 and 2 for pat.

K4, P4 Rib (multiple of 8 sts + 4)
Row 1 (RS): K4, *p4, k4; rep from * across.
Row 2: P4, *k4, p4; rep from * across.
Rep Rows 1 and 2 for pat.

Cable Panel (4-st panel)
Rows 1 and 5 (RS): K4.
Row 2 and all WS rows: P4.
Row 3: 2/2 RC.
Row 6: P4.
Rep Rows 1–6 for pat.

Special Techniques
Provisional Cast-On: With crochet hook and waste yarn, make a chain several sts longer than desired cast-on. With knitting needle and project yarn, pick up indicated number of sts in "bumps" on back of chain. When indicated in pat, "unzip" the crochet chain to free live sts.

3-Needle Bind-Off: With pieces arranged as specified in pat and needles parallel, using a 3rd needle, knit tog a st from front needle with 1 st from back needle. *Knit tog a st from front and back needles, and slip the first st over the 2nd to bind off. Rep from * across, then fasten off last st.

Pattern Notes
When shaping sleeves, work increases 1 stitch from each edge using M1 increase. Work decreases 1 stitch from each edge as slip, slip, knit (ssk) at beginning of row and knit 2 together (k2tog) at end of row.

The lower back body and upper body/collar are worked from side to side and are shaped with short rows, bringing new stitches gradually into work at the beginning and working fewer stitches each row at the end. There is no need to wrap the stitches at the short-row turns.

The upper and lower body sections are joined so that the right side (RS) of lower body and the wrong side (WS) of upper body appear to be facing out. When worn, the collar will be turned back so that the RS is showing.

Sleeve & Yoke
Cast on 30 (34, 38, 42, 46) sts.

Work K2, P2 Rib and inc 1 st at each edge [every 6 rows] 12 times, working new sts into rib as they accumulate—54 (58, 62, 66, 70) sts.

Work even until sleeve measures 20 (19, 18, 17, 17) inches. Place markers at each side to indicate beg of yoke.

Work even until yoke measures 20 (22, 24, 26, 28) inches from markers. Place markers at each side to indicate beg of 2nd sleeve.

Work even for approx 0 (0, 1, 2, 3) inch(es).

Dec at each edge of next row, then [every 6 rows] 11 times—30 (34, 38, 42, 46) sts.

When 2nd sleeve measures same as first sleeve, bind off loosely in pat.

Lower Back Body
Using Provisional Cast-On, cast on 52 (52, 60, 60, 68) sts.

Short-row shaping

Rows 1 (RS) and 2: K4 sts, turn. P4.

Rows 3 and 4: K4, p4, turn. K4, p4.

Rows 5 and 6: 2/2 RC, p4, k4, turn. P4, k4, p4.

Continue working 4 more sts every RS row, maintaining Cable Panel at beg of row and working new sts into K4, P4 Rib until there are enough rows to make cable turns on the knit sts. K4, P4 Rib will become Cable 4, p4 across.

When all sts have been worked, place marker for first underarm placement.

Work even in cabled ribbing until straight section measures 20 (22, 24, 26, 28) inches.

Place marker for 2nd underarm.

Decrease using short rows as follows:

Maintain pat and on WS rows, work 4 fewer sts each row until 4 sts remain.

Put all sts on waste yarn or spare circular needle.

Upper Body/Collar

Work as for lower back body, but work only 1 cable at beg of row (long edge), and all other sts in rev St st.

Finishing

Weave in ends. Block pieces.

Unzip Provisional Cast-On for lower body and place live sts on circular needle.

With WS of lower body and RS (rev St st side) of upper body/collar facing you, join cast-on edge of lower body and dec edge of collar using 3-Needle Bind-Off. Alternatively, join with Kitchener st (see page 47) with RS of lower body and WS of upper body/collar facing.

Rep on other side.

Sew sleeve seams from cuff to markers.

Join non-cabled straight edge of body to yoke edge using mattress st.

To wear: Fold upper body/collar to outside. ●

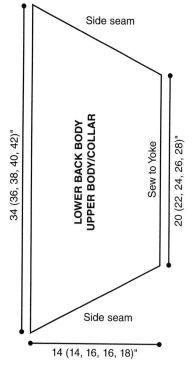

Side seam

LOWER BACK BODY
UPPER BODY/COLLAR

Sew to Yoke

34 (36, 38, 40, 42)"

20 (22, 24, 26, 28)"

Side seam

14 (14, 16, 16, 18)"

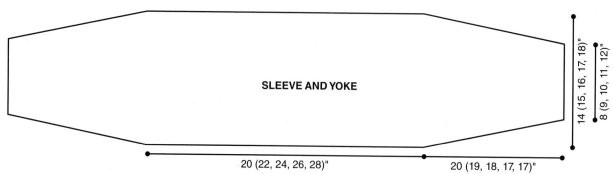

SLEEVE AND YOKE

14 (15, 16, 17, 18)"

8 (9, 10, 11, 12)"

20 (22, 24, 26, 28)"

20 (19, 18, 17, 17)"

Urban Flats

Elegant undulating cables accentuate the drama of this long, flowing jacket.

Design by Nancy Rieck

Skill Level
■ ■ ■ ■ ☐ EXPERIENCED

Sizes
Woman's small (medium, large, extra-large, 2X-large) Instructions are given for smallest size, with larger sizes in parentheses. When only 1 number is given, it applies to all sizes.

Finished Measurements
Chest: Customized
Note: Yarn amounts are given for chest circumferences of 36 (40, 44, 48, 52) inches.
Length: Customized

Materials

- Cascade Yarns Eco Alpaca (DK weight; 100% undyed baby alpaca; 220 yds/100g per ball): 9 (10, 12, 14, 15) balls beige #1511
- Size 4 (3.5mm) double-point (set of 5), 16- and 32-inch (or longer) circular needles or size needed to obtain gauge
- Size 5 (3.75mm) 32-inch (or longer) circular needle
- Size F/5 (3.75mm) crochet hook
- Cable needle
- Stitch markers
- Stitch holders (cable-type or waste yarn)

Gauge
24 sts and 28 rows = 4 inches/10cm in St st.

56 sts and 24 rows = 4½ x 3½ inches in Cable pat (1 rep).

To save time, take time to check gauge.

Special Abbreviations
12 over 12 Left Ribbed Cross (12/12 LRC): Sl 12 to cn and hold in front; [k2, p2] 3 times; [k2, p2] 3 times from cn.

12 over 12 Right Ribbed Cross (12/12 RRC): Sl 12 to cn and hold in back; [k2, p2] 3 times; [k2, p2] 3 times from cn.

Place marker (pm): Place marker on needle.

Slip marker (sm): Slip marker from LH needle to RH needle.

Lifted Increase (LI): K1 in top of st in row below next st on LH needle.

Lifted Increase-Purl (LI-P): P1 in top of st in row below next st on LH needle.

Right Twist (RT): K2tog leaving sts on LH needle, knit into first st on needle, slip both sts from needle.

Special Techniques

Provisional Cast-On: With crochet hook and waste yarn, make a chain several sts longer than desired cast-on. With knitting needle and project yarn, pick up indicated number of sts in the "bumps" on back of chain. When indicated in pattern, "unzip" the crochet chain to free live sts.

RT I-Cord Bind-Off: Cast on 3 sts. *RT, ssk, sl 3 back to LH needle; k2, ssk, sl 3 back to LH needle; rep from * to last 3 sts, sl 1, ssk, pass the first st over the 2nd st.

Pattern Stitch

Cable (56-st panel)
Rows 1, 3, 5, 7, 11, 13, 15, 17, 19, and 23 (RS): K3, p2, *k2, p2; rep from * to last 3 sts, k3.
Row 2 and all WS rows: P3, k2, *p2, k2; rep from * to last 3 sts, p3.
Row 9: K3, p2, 12/12 LRC, *k2, p2; rep from * to last 3 sts, k3.
Row 21: K3, p2, *k2, p2; rep from * to last 27 sts, 12/12 RRC, k3.
Row 24: Rep Row 2.
Rep Rows 1–24 for pat.

Pattern Notes

Knitter customizes sizing to fit herself as desired.

Sweater is worked in one piece with raglan shaping, beginning with the cabled back collar. Stitches are picked up along side edge of back collar to begin the yoke, which is worked to the underarm, at which point the body and sleeves are worked separately.

When picking up stitches, pick up 1 stitch in each row.

Change to longer or shorter circular or double-point needles for body and sleeve as needed to accommodate stitches.

The baby alpaca yarn gives the sweater its wonderful drape. However, it will "grow" when garment is blocked and worn, so work the body shorter than desired length, and then block to finished length.

Back Collar

Using Provisional Cast-On, cast on 56 sts.

Beg with Row 5, work 44 rows in Cable pat, ending with Row 24.

Cut yarn and place sts on holder or waste yarn.

Unzip Provisional Cast-On and slip 56 live sts to needle.

With RS facing and beg with Row 5, work 43 rows in Cable pat, ending with Row 23.

Cut yarn and place sts on holder or waste yarn.

Yoke

Pick-up row (RS): Turn collar sideways so that end just completed is at your right. Count 10 rows from the right end along the top edge. With new yarn, pick up and knit 64 sts in next 64 rows—10 rows rem at left end.

Set-up row (WS): P2 [right front], pm; p10 (8, 6, 4, 4) [right sleeve], pm; p40 (44, 48, 52, 52) [back], pm; p10 (8, 6, 4, 4) [left sleeve], pm; p2, pick up and purl 2 sts [left front]—66 sts.

Row 1: K3, LI, k1, *k4, LI, knit to 4 sts before marker, LI, k4, sm; rep from * twice, k1, LI, k1, pick up and knit 2 sts—76 sts with 8 raglan incs and 2 more sts at right front edge.

Rows 2, 4, 6 and 8: Purl to end, pick up and purl 2 sts—2 more sts at left front edge.

Row 3: Knit to 2 sts before marker, LI, k2, sm, *k5, LI, knit to 5 sts before marker, LI, k5, sm; rep from * twice, k2, LI, knit to end, pick up and knit 2 sts—88 sts.

Row 5: *Knit to 1 st before marker, LI, k1, sm, k1, LI; rep from * 3 times, knit to end, pick up and knit 2 sts—100 sts.

Row 7: *Knit to 2 sts before marker, LI, k2, sm, k2, LI; rep from * 3 times, knit to end, pick up and knit 2 sts—102 sts.

Row 9: *Knit to 3 sts before marker, LI, k3, sm, k3, LI; rep from * 3 times, knit to end, pick up and knit 2 sts—124 sts.

Row 10: Purl to end; transfer 56 sts from waste yarn to LH needle and work Row 24 of Cable pat across—180 sts.

Row 11: Work Row 1 of Cable pat, *knit to 4 sts before marker, LI, k4, sm, k4, LI; rep from * 3 times, knit to end, transfer 56 sts from waste yarn to LH needle and work Row 1 of Cable pat—244 sts with 56 Cable pat sts at each edge.

Row 12 and all WS rows to end of yoke: Work Cable pat, purl to last 56 sts, work Cable pat.

Continue Cable pat at each edge to end of sweater body.

Row 13: *Work to 5 sts before marker, LI, k5, sm, k5, LI; rep from * 3 times, work to end—252 sts.

Row 15: *Work to 1 st before marker, LI, k1, sm, k1, LI; rep from * 3 times, work to end—260 sts.

Row 17: *Work to 2 sts before marker, LI, k2, sm, k2, LI; rep from * 3 times, work to end—268 sts.

Row 19: *Work to 3 sts before marker, LI, k3, sm, k3, LI; rep from * 3 times, knit work to end—276 sts.

Row 21: *Work to 4 sts before marker, LI, k4, sm, k4, LI; rep from * 3 times, work to end—284 sts.

Row 23: *Work to 5 sts before marker, LI, k5, sm, k5, LI; rep from * 3 times, work to end—292 sts, with 56 Cable sts each side, 24 sts each front, 34 (32, 30, 28, 28) sts each sleeve and 40 (44, 48, 52, 52) back sts.

Row 24: Work even.

Continue to inc, following sequence established in Rows 15–24 until body and sleeves fit you.

Notes for Custom Fitting Yoke
The size of your sweater will depend on how many inc rows you work for the yoke.

Place your sts on a piece of waste yarn that is long enough to give you plenty of ease. Try your sweater on to see how much deeper your yoke should be. Decide whether you need more or fewer sts for the body or sleeves, or more or fewer rows before the underarm join, modifying as necessary. *Note: Bear in mind that you will be casting on extra underarm sts at your body join and sleeve area, so account for this.* The completed yoke should hit you a few inches below your armpit. When a section (body or sleeves) fits you, stop increasing in that section. If you want the yoke to be longer, work even until it's the desired length.

Divide body & sleeves

Division row (RS): Removing markers as you come to them, *work across left front sts, cast on 6 (6, 8, 8, 10) underarm sts, place left sleeve sts on waste yarn; rep from * across back and right sleeve sts, work right front. Count body sts and pm at center back.

Work even for 1 inch.

Back Rib Inset
Row 1 (RS): Work to marker at center back, LI-P, pm, work to end—1 st inc.

Rows 2 and 4: Work to marker, sm, k1, sm, work to end.

Row 3: Work to marker, sm, p1, sm, work to end.

Row 5: Work to marker, sm, LI-P, p1, sm, work to end.

Rows 6, 8 and 10: Work to marker, sm, k2, sm, work to end.

Rows 7 and 9: Work to marker, sm, p2, sm, work to end.

Row 11: Work to 2 sts before marker, pm, LI-P, k2 remove marker, p2, remove marker, k2, LI-P, pm, work to end.

Rows 12, 14, 16 and 18: Work in established pat, working rib across marked center back sts.

Row 13: Work to marker, sm, LI-P, p1, k2, p2, k2, LI-P, p1, sm, work to end.

Rows 15 and 17: Work in established pat, working rib across marked center back sts.

Rep [Rows 11–18] 3 more times.

Change to larger needles and rep [Rows 11–18] 3 more times, then work even until sweater measures approx 4 inches short of desired wearing length *(see Pattern Notes).*

Bind off all sts using RT I-Cord Bind-Off.

Sleeves
Transfer sleeve sts from waste yarn to 16-inch circular or dpns.

Pick up and knit 6 (6, 8, 8, 10) sts along body underarm, placing marker in center of underarm for beg of rnd.

Work in St st for 6 inches.

Dec rnd: K1, ssk, work to last 3 sts, k2tog, k1— 2 sts dec.

Rep Dec rnd [every 4 (4, 3, 3, 3) rnds 7 (8, 9, 10, 11) more times—14 (16, 18, 20, 22) sts dec.

Sleeve rib inset
Count sleeve sts and pm at center top of sleeve.

Rnds 1–4: Knit to marker, sm, p1, knit to end.

Rnds 5–10: Knit to marker, sm, p2, pm, knit to end.

Rnd 11: Knit to 2 sts before marker, pm, LI-P, k2, remove marker, p2, k2, LI-P, pm, knit to end— 2 sts inc.

Rnd 12: Work the sts as they present themselves.

Rnd 13: Knit to marker, sm, LI-P, work in established rib to 1 st before next marker, LI-P, p1, sm, knit to end—2 sts inc.

Rnds 14–18: Rep Rnd 12.

Rep [Rnds 11–18] twice more—8 sts inc.

Work even until sleeve measures desired length from underarm.

Bind off all sts using RT I-Cord Bind-Off.

Finishing
Weave in all ends. Block sweater to desired size. •

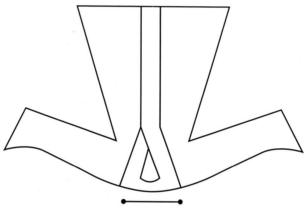

6¾ (7¼, 8, 8¾, 8¾)"

Note: All other measurements are customized by knitter.

STITCH KEY

☐ K on RS, p on WS
⊟ P on RS, k on WS

12/12 LRC
12/12 RRC

CABLE PANEL

56-st panel

Diamond Cabled Cardi

A girl can't resist the luxury of diamonds. Go on and spoil yourself with this stylish and comfortable cover-up with unique cablework.

Design by Tabetha Hedrick

Skill Level

◼◼◼◻ INTERMEDIATE

Sizes

Woman's small (medium, large, extra-large, 2X-large) Instructions are given for smallest size, with larger sizes in parentheses. When only 1 number is given, it applies to all sizes. When a zero is used, no stitches are worked for that size.

Finished Measurements

Chest: 37 (41, 45, 49, 53) inches
Length: approx 23¾ (24¼, 25, 25¼, 26¼) inches

Materials

- Austermann Natura (worsted weight; 46% wool/28% bamboo/12% cotton/7% alpaca/7% mohair; 109 yds/50g per ball): 9 (10, 10, 10, 11) balls eggplant #15
- Size 9 (5.5mm) straight and 32-inch circular needles or size needed to obtain finished gauge
- Cable needle

[4 MEDIUM]

Gauge

16 sts and 25½ rows = 4 inches/10cm in St st (washed and blocked).

17 sts and 27½ rows = 4 inches/10cm in Diamond Cable pat (washed and blocked).

To save time, take time to check gauge over blocked swatch.

Special Abbreviations

1 over 1 Right Cross (1/1 RC): Sl 1 to cn and hold in back, k1, k1 from cn.

1 over 1 Left Cross (1/1 LC): Sl 1 to cn and hold in front, k1, k1 from cn.

1 over 1 Left Purl Cross (1/1 LPC): Sl 1 to cn and hold in front, p1, k1 from cn.

1 over 1 Right Purl Cross (1/1 RPC): Sl 1 to cn and hold in back, k1, p1 from cn.

Pattern Stitches
K2, P2, Rib (multiple of 4 sts + 6)
Row 1 (RS): K3, p2, *k2, p2; rep from * to last st, k1.
Rep Row 1 for pat.

Diamond Cable (multiple of 8 sts + 14)
Row 1 (RS): K1, p5, 1/1 RC, *p6, 1/1 RC; rep from * to last 6 sts, p5, k1.
Row 2: K6, p2, *k6, p2; rep from * to last 6 sts, k6.
Row 3: K1, p4, *1/1 RC, 1/1 LC, p4; rep from * to last st, k1.
Row 4: K5, *p4, k4; rep from * to last st, k1.
Row 5: K1, p3, *1/1 RC, k2, 1/1 LC, p2; rep from * to last 2 sts, p1, k1.
Row 6: K4, *p6, k2; rep from * to last 2 sts, k2.
Row 7: K1, p2, *1/1 RC, k4, 1/1 LC; rep from * to last 3 sts, p2, k1.
Row 8: K1, purl to last st, k1.
Row 9: K2, 1/1 RC, *k6, 1/1 RC; rep from * to last 2 sts, k2.
Row 10: Rep Row 8.
Row 11: K1, p2, *1/1 LPC, k4, 1/1 RPC; rep from * to last 3 sts, p2, k1.
Row 12: Rep Row 6.
Row 13: K1, p3, *1/1 LPC, k2, 1/1 RPC; rep from * to last 2 sts, p1, k1.
Row 14: Rep Row 4.
Row 15: K1, p4, *1/1 LPC, 1/1 RPC, p4; rep from * to last st, k1.
Row 16: Rep Row 2.
Rep Rows 1–16 for pat.

Pattern Note
Raglan armhole and front neck shaping are worked at the same time.

Back
Cast on 74 (82, 90, 98, 106) sts.

Work K2, P2 Rib for 6 rows.

Change to St st and work even until back measures 15¾ (15¾, 16, 16, 16¼) inches, ending with a WS row.

Shape raglan
Bind off 5 (5, 6, 6, 9) sts at beg of next 2 rows—64 (72, 78, 86, 88) sts.

Dec row (RS): K1, ssk, knit to last 3 sts, k2tog, k1—62 (70, 76, 84, 86) sts.

Work 3 rows even.

Rep [last 4 rows] 4 (2, 1, 0, 0) time(s) more—54 (66, 74, 84, 86) sts.

Rep Dec row [every RS row] 16 (21, 25, 29, 30) times—22 (24, 24, 26, 26) sts.

Bind off rem sts for back neck.

Left Front
Cast on 46 (54, 54, 62, 62) sts.

Work Diamond Cable pat until left front measures 15¾ (15¾, 16, 16, 16¼) inches, ending with a WS row.

Shape raglan & neck
Note: Raglan and neck shaping are worked at the same time.

Bind off 5 (5, 6, 6, 9) sts at beg of next row—41 (49, 48, 56, 53) sts rem.

Raglan dec row (RS): K1, ssk (armhole dec), work in established pat to end.

Work 3 rows even at raglan edge.

Rep [last 4 rows] 4 (2, 1, 0, 0) time(s) more, then rep Raglan dec row [every RS row] 16 (21, 25, 29, 30) times.

At the same time, work neck shaping as follows:

Neck dec row (RS): Work in established pat to last 3 sts, k2tog (neck dec), k1.

Work 3 rows even at neck edge.

Rep [last 4 rows] 7 (3, 9, 5, 11) times more, then rep Neck dec row [every RS row] 10 (19, 9, 18, 8) times.

Bind off rem 2 sts on next RS row.

Right Front
Cast on 46 (54, 54, 62, 62) sts.

Work Diamond Cable pat until right front measures 15¾ (15¾, 16, 16, 16¼) inches, ending with a RS row.

Shape raglan & neck
Note: Raglan and neck shaping are worked at the same time.

Bind off 5 (5, 6, 6, 9) sts at beg of next row—41 (49, 48, 56, 53) sts rem.

Neck dec row (RS): K1, ssk (neck dec), work in established pat to end.

Work 3 rows even at neck edge.

Rep [last 4 rows] 7 (3, 9, 5, 11) times more, then rep Dec row [every RS row] 10 (19, 9, 18, 8) times.

At the same time, work raglan shaping as follows:

Raglan dec row (RS): Work in established pat to last 3 sts, k2tog (armhole dec), k1.

Work 3 rows even at raglan edge.

Rep [last 4 rows] 4 (2, 1, 0, 0) time(s) more, then rep Raglan dec row [every RS row] 16 (21, 25, 29, 30) times.

Bind off rem 2 sts on next RS row.

Sleeves
Cast on 66 (70, 74, 82, 90) sts.

Work K2, P2 Rib for 6 rows.

Change to St st and work even until sleeve measures 5 (5, 5¾, 5¾, 6¾) inches, ending with a WS row.

Shape raglan
Bind off 5 (5, 6, 6, 9) sts at beg of next 2 rows— 56 (60, 62, 70, 72) sts.

Dec row (RS): K1, ssk, knit to last 3 sts, k2tog, k1—54 (58, 60, 68, 70) sts.

Work 3 rows even.

Rep [last 4 rows] 4 (3, 4, 4, 4) times more—46 (52, 52, 60, 62) sts.

Rep Dec row [every RS row] 16 (19, 19, 21, 22) times—14 (14, 14, 18, 18) sts.

Bind off rem sts.

Finishing
Weave in ends. Block pieces to finished measurements.

Sew sleeve caps to raglan armholes. Sew side and sleeve seams.

Neck Band
With RS facing and using circular needle, beg at lower edge of front, pick up and knit 117 (120, 124, 125, 129) sts evenly along right front edge, 14 (14, 14, 18, 18) sts from sleeve cap, 22 (24, 24, 26, 26) sts from back neck and 117 (120, 124, 125, 129) sts along left front edge—284 (292, 300, 312, 320) sts.

Row 1 (WS): Sl 1, *k2, p2; rep from * to last 3 sts, k3.

Row 2 (RS): Sl 1, *p2, k2; rep from * to last 3 sts, p2, k1.

Rep Rows 1 and 2 until band measures 4 inches, ending with a WS row.

Bind off loosely kwise.

Weave in ends and block neck band lightly. ●

STITCH KEY

☐ K on RS, p on WS
– P on RS, k on WS
⤬ 1/1 RC
⤬ 1/1 LC
⤬ 1/1 RPC
⤬ 1/1 LPC

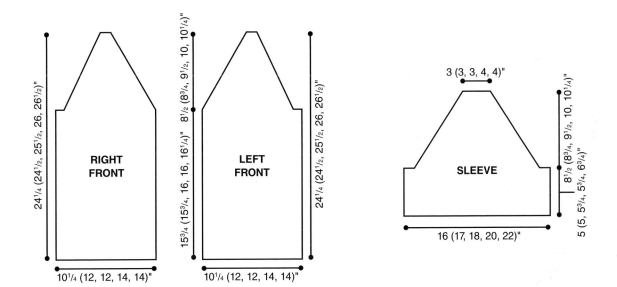

8-st rep

DIAMOND CABLE

RIGHT FRONT

24¼ (24½, 25½, 26, 26½)"

8½ (8¾, 9½, 10, 10¼)"

15¾ (15¾, 16, 16, 16¼)"

10¼ (12, 12, 14, 14)"

LEFT FRONT

24¼ (24½, 25½, 26, 26½)"

10¼ (12, 12, 14, 14)"

SLEEVE

3 (3, 3, 4, 4)"

8½ (8¾, 9½, 10, 10¼)"

5 (5, 5¾, 5¾, 6¾)"

16 (17, 18, 20, 22)"

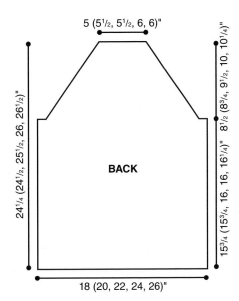

BACK

5 (5½, 5½, 6, 6)"

24¼ (24½, 25½, 26, 26½)"

8½ (8¾, 9½, 10, 10¼)"

15¾ (15¾, 16, 16, 16¼)"

18 (20, 22, 24, 26)"

Celtic Kimono

Feel the echo of the past with this delightfully textured sweater that combines thoroughly modern styling with a Celtic cable motif.

Design by Lynne LeBlanc

. . . .

Skill Level

◼◼◼◼ EXPERIENCED

Sizes

Woman's small (medium/large, extra-large/2X-large) Instructions are given for smallest size, with larger sizes in parentheses. When only 1 number is given, it applies to all sizes.

Finished Measurements

Chest: 44 (49¼, 54½) inches (buttoned)
Length: 27½ (29¼, 31½) inches

Materials

• Rowan Pure Wool Aran (Aran weight; 100% superwash wool; 186 yds/100g per skein): 14 (16, 19) skeins cedar #674
• Size 4 (3.5mm) 24- and 40-inch circular needles
• Size 5 (3.75mm) 24- and 40-inch circular needles or size needed to obtain gauge
• Size 6 (4mm) 24- and 40-inch circular needles or size needed to obtain gauge
• Size G/6 (4mm) crochet hook
• Size H/8 (5mm) crochet hook
• Cable needle
• Stitch markers
• Stitch holders
• 2 [1¼-inch] buttons*

Outer button on sample is #93363 Berry Leaves in Antique Silver from The Nicky Epstein Collection by JHB International; inner button can be any button.

Gauge

18 sts and 24 rows = 4 inches/10cm in St st with size 5 needle.

24 sts and 28 rows = 4 inches/10cm in Trinity St with size 6 needle.

To save time, take time to check gauge.

Special Abbreviations

3 over 1 Right Purl Cross (3/1 RPC): Sl 1 to cn and hold in back, k3, p1 from cn.

3 over 1 Left Purl Cross (3/1 LPC): Sl 3 to cn and hold in front, p1, k3 from cn.

3 over 2 Right Purl Cross (3/2 RPC): Sl 2 to cn and hold in back, k3, p2 from cn.

3 over 2 Left Purl Cross (3/2 LPC): Sl 3 to cn and hold in front, p2, k3 from cn.

3 over 3 Right Cross (3/3 RC): Sl 3 to cn and hold in back, k3, k3 from cn.

3 over 3 Left Cross (3/3 LC): Sl 3 to cn and hold in front, k3, k3 from cn.

7 sts-into-one (Dec6): Sl 4 sts to RH needle wyif, drop yarn; *pass 2nd st on RH needle over first st on RH needle; slip first st from RH needle back to LH needle; pass 2nd st on LH needle over first st on LH needle**; slip first st from LH needle back to RH needle and rep from * to ** twice more; pick up yarn and purl rem st.

Make 1 Left (M1L): Insert LH needle from front to back under the running thread between the last st worked and next st on LH needle; knit into the back of resulting loop.

Make 1 Right (M1R): Insert LH needle from back to front under the running thread between the last st worked and next st on LH needle. With RH needle, knit into the front of resulting loop.

S2KP2: Sl 2 as if to k2tog, k1, pass slipped sts over—a centered double-dec.

Pattern Stitches

Trinity St (multiple of 4 sts)
Rows 1 and 3 (RS): *P4; rep from * across.
Row 2: *[K1, p1, k1] in same st, p3tog; rep from * across.
Row 4: *P3tog, [k1, p1, k1] in same st; rep from * across.

Cable Panel (20-st [inc to 26-st] panel)
Row 1 (RS): P1, k3, p12, k3, p1.
Row 2 and all WS rows except Row 4: Work sts as they present themselves.
Row 3: P1, k3, p3, M1, [k1, k1-tbl, k1] in next st, M1, p6, k3, p1—24 sts.
Row 4: K1, p3, k6, p2, [p1, yo, p1] in next st, p2, k5, p3, k1—26 sts.
Row 5: P1, k3, p4, 3/1 RPC, k1, 3/2 LPC, p4, k3, p1.
Row 7: P1, k3, p3, 3/1 RPC, p4, 3/2 LPC, 3/2 RPC, p1.
Row 9: P1, k3, p3, k3, p7, 3/3 LC, p3.
Row 11: P1, k3, p3, 3/1 LPC, p4, 3/2 RPC, 3/2 LPC, p1.
Row 13: P1, k3, p4, 3/2 LPC, 3/2 RPC, p4, k3, p1.
Row 15: P1, k3, p6, 3/3 RC, p6, k3, p1.
Row 17: P1, k3, p4, 3/2 RPC, 3/2 LPC, p4, k3, p1.
Row 19: P1, 3/2 LPC, 3/2 RPC, p4, 3/1 LPC, p3, k3, p1.
Row 21: P3, 3/3 LC, p7, k3, p3, k3, p1.
Row 23: P1, 3/2 RPC, 3/2 LPC, p4, 3/1 RPC, p3, k3, p1.
Row 25: P1, k3, p4, 3/2 LPC, p1, 3/1 RPC, p4, k3, p1.
Row 27: P1, k3, p6, Dec6, p5, k3, p1—20 sts.
Row 28: Work as for Row 2.
Rep Rows 1–28 for pat.

Special Technique

Provisional Cast-On: With smaller crochet hook and waste yarn, make a chain several sts longer than desired cast-on. With knitting needle and project yarn, pick up indicated number of sts in the "bumps" on back of chain. When indicated in pat, "unzip" the crochet chain and place live sts on needle.

Pattern Notes

The sweater is worked in 1 piece to the pocket opening, and then worked in 3 sections simultaneously. The sections are rejoined and worked to the underarm, at which point the fronts and back are worked simultaneously. If desired, each section can be worked separately with the other sections on hold.

When shaping, if there are not enough stitches to work the 4-stitch Trinity Stitch, work the extra stitches in reverse stockinette stitch.

The inner hem is worked on size 4 needles to keep hem from splaying. If desired for sharper hem turn, work turning ridge (knit across on wrong side) before changing needles.

The stitch count for the Cable Panel starts at 20 stitches, increases to 26 stitches and decreases back down to 20 stitches. When counting stitches, always count each Cable Panel as 20 stitches, even when there are 26 stitches.

When binding off the Cable Panel, you must decrease back down to 20 sts as follows: Work the inner 2 [k3] ribs as k3tog and/or work p2tog twice in the purl sections at the same time that you are binding off—0, 4 or 6 stitches decreased, as needed, depending on what row you are on.

Body

Hem

With size 4 needle, using Provisional Cast-On, cast on 250 (290, 330) sts.

Work in St st for 1½ inches.

Change to size 5 needle and work in St st for 1½ inches, ending with a WS row.

Unzip Provisional Cast-On and put live sts on smallest needle.

Joining row (RS): Holding both needles parallel and with size 5 needle in front, knit 1 front st tog with 1 back st across.

Inc row (WS): Change to size 6 needle and inc 52 (60, 68) sts evenly across—302 (350, 398) sts.

Main section

Row 1 (set-up, RS): P9 (17, 25), work Row 1 of Cable Panel across 20 sts, p16 (20, 24) sts, work Cable Panel, pm, p40 (48, 56), [work Cable Panel, p16 (20, 24)] twice, work Cable Panel, p40 (48, 56), pm, work Cable Panel, p16 (20, 24) sts, work Cable Panel, p9 (17, 25) sts—300 (344, 396) sts, with 2 Cable Panels on each front and 3 Cable Panels on back.

Row 2: K1 (edge st), work Row 2 of Trinity St across 8 (16, 24) sts, work Cable Panel, work Trinity St across 16 (20, 24) sts, work Cable Panel, work Trinity St across 36 (44, 56) sts, [work Cable Panel, work Trinity St across 16 (20, 24) sts] twice, work Cable Panel, work Trinity St across 36 (44, 56) sts, work Cable Panel, work Trinity St across 16 (20, 24) sts, work Cable Panel, work Trinity St across 8 (16, 24) sts, k1 (edge st).

Maintaining edge sts in rev St st, work even in established pats until piece measures 7½ (8, 8½) inches, ending with a WS row.

Divide for pockets (RS): Work to marker, M1L for selvage st, remove marker; join 2nd ball of yarn, work in pat to next marker, remove marker; join 3rd ball of yarn, M1L for selvage st, then work to end— 2 selvage sts added.

Working the 3 sections at once, work even until piece measures 12½ (13, 14) inches, ending with a WS row.

Joining row (RS): Using 1 ball of yarn, work in pat across all sts and p2tog at each join to eliminate the selvage sts.

Work even until piece measures 19½ (20½, 22) inches, ending with a WS row.

Shape armholes

Row 1 (RS): Work to end of 2nd Cable Panel, p13 (16, 19), join 2nd ball of yarn and bind off 14 (16, 18) sts for underarm, work to end of 3rd back Cable Panel, p13 (16, 19); join 3rd ball of yarn and bind off 14 (16, 18) sts for underarm, work in pat to end—78 (93, 108) sts each front and 118 (132, 146) back sts.

Next 2 rows: Work across front; bind off 4 (5, 6) sts at back armhole edge, then work across back; bind off 4 (5, 6) sts at front armhole edge, work to end—74 (88, 102) sts each front and 110 (122, 134) back sts.

Next 2 rows: Work across front; bind off 2 (3, 5) sts at back armhole edge, then work across back; bind off 2 (3, 5) sts at front armhole edge, work to end—72 (85, 97) sts each front and 106 (116, 124) back sts.

Dec row (WS): Work to 3 sts before armhole edge, k2tog, k1; k1, ssk, work to 3 sts before armhole edge, k2tog, k1; k1, ssk, work to end—71 (84, 96) sts each front; 104 (114, 122) back sts.

Dec row (RS): Work to 3 sts before armhole edge, ssp, p1; p1, p2tog, work to 3 sts before armhole edge, ssp, p1; p1, p2tog, work to end—70 (83, 95) sts each front; 102 (112, 120) back sts.

Dec at armhole edges [every other row] 3 (4, 4) more times—67 (79, 91) sts each front; 96 (104, 112) back sts.

Work even until front armholes measure approx 3¾ inches, ending with a WS row. If desired, put back sts on holder while working front necks, then continue back when done with fronts.

Front neck

Bind off at each neck edge 8 (10, 14) sts once, 4 sts 2 (3, 3) times, 3 sts 3 times, 2 sts 5 (6, 8) times, then dec 1 st at neck edge [every row] 7 (8, 9) times—25 (28, 31) sts rem each shoulder.

Work even until armholes measure 8 (8¾, 9½) inches.

Bind off at each shoulder 13 (14, 16) sts once, then 12 (14, 15) sts once.

Shape back neck & shoulders

At the same time, work back even until armholes measure approx 7¼ (8, 8¾) inches, ending with a WS row.

Row 1 (RS): Work 33 (36, 39) sts, join a new ball of yarn and bind off center 30 (32, 34) sts, work to end.

Working each side separately, bind off 4 sts at each neck edge twice—25 (28, 31) sts each shoulder.

Bind off 13 (14, 16) sts at beg of next 2 rows, then bind off 12 (14, 15) sts at beg of following 2 rows.

Sleeves

Hem

With size 4 needle, using Provisional Cast-On, cast on 45 (52, 56) sts.

Work in St st for 1¾ inches.

Change to size 5 needle and continue in St st for 1¾ inches, ending with a WS row.

Unzip Provisional Cast-On and put live sts on size 4 needle.

Joining row (RS): Holding both sets of needles parallel with size 5 needle in front, knit 1 front st tog with 1 back st across.

Inc row (WS): Change to size 6 needle and inc 15 (18, 20) sts evenly spaced across row—60 (70, 76) sts.

Main section

Row 1 (set-up, RS): P2 (5, 6), work Cable Panel over 20 sts, p16 (20, 24), work Cable Panel over 20 sts, p2 (5, 6).

Row 2: K2 (1, 2), work Trinity St over 0 (4, 4) sts, work Cable Panel, work Row 2 of Trinity St over 16 (20, 24) sts, work Cable Panel, work Trinity St over 0 (4, 4) sts, k2 (1, 2).

Maintaining 1 st each side in rev St st for selvage, work even for 2 rows.

Inc 1 st each side inside selvage sts on next row, then [every 4 rows] 3 (5, 13) times, and then [every 6 rows] 14 (13, 8) times, working new sts into Trinity St as they accumulate—96 (108, 120) sts.

Work even until sleeve measures 17 (17½, 18) inches or desired length, ending with a WS row.

Sleeve cap

Note: Remember to dec while binding off Cable Panels as necessary (see Pattern Notes).

Bind off 7 (8, 9) sts at beg of next 2 rows—82 (92, 102) sts.

Bind off 3 sts at beg of next 6 (6, 10) rows—64 (74, 72) sts.

Bind off 4 sts at beg of next 4 rows—48 (58, 56) sts.

Bind off 6 sts at beg of next 2 (4, 4) rows—36 (34, 32) sts.

Bind off rem sts.

Finishing

Pocket lining
With size 5 needle, cast on 44 (52, 60) sts.

Work 11 (11½, 12½) inches in St st.

Bind off.

Pocket opening hem
With size 5 needle, pick up and knit 23 (23, 25) sts along Cable Panel at front edge of pocket opening.

Work 1¼ inches in St st.

Change size 4 needle and work 1¼ inches in St st.

Fold in half with WS tog; sew live sts to first row of picked-up sts.

Sew sides of hem to body of sweater, going through both layers.

Weave in all ends. Block all pieces to finished measurements.

Sew shoulder seams.

Sew sleeves to body; sew sleeve seams.

Front & neck band
With RS facing and using size 6 needle, pick up and knit along right front, around neck and along left front, picking up approx 3 sts for every 5 rows and 3 sts for every 4 sts in main fabric, placing markers in corner sts where front band turns to neck. *Note: When picking up in bottom hem, pick up in RS fabric only.*

Row 1 (WS): Purl.

Row 2 (RS): *Knit to 1 st before marked corner st, M1L, knit corner st, M1R; rep from * once, knit to end.

Rows 3–5: Work in St st.

Row 6: Rep Row 2.

Rows 7–9: Work in St st.

Rows 10 and 11: Change to size 4 needle and work in St st.

Row 12: *Knit to 1 st before corner st, S2KP2; rep from * once, knit to end.

Rows 13–15: Work in St st.

Row 16: Rep Row 12.

Rows 17–19: Work in St st.

Whipstitch live sts to body, aligning sts with picked-up sts so that hem isn't skewed.

Sew all 4 sides of pocket lining to body of garment starting at lower front edge at hem join.

Weave in rem ends.

Using larger crochet hook and double strand of yarn, make 1-inch chain at each front neck corner for button loops; weave in ends securely.

Sew buttons to right and left sides of body, positioning for correct fit with overlapping fronts. ●

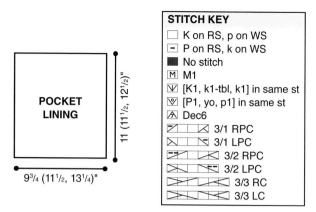

POCKET LINING

11 (11½, 12½)"

9¾ (11½, 13¼)"

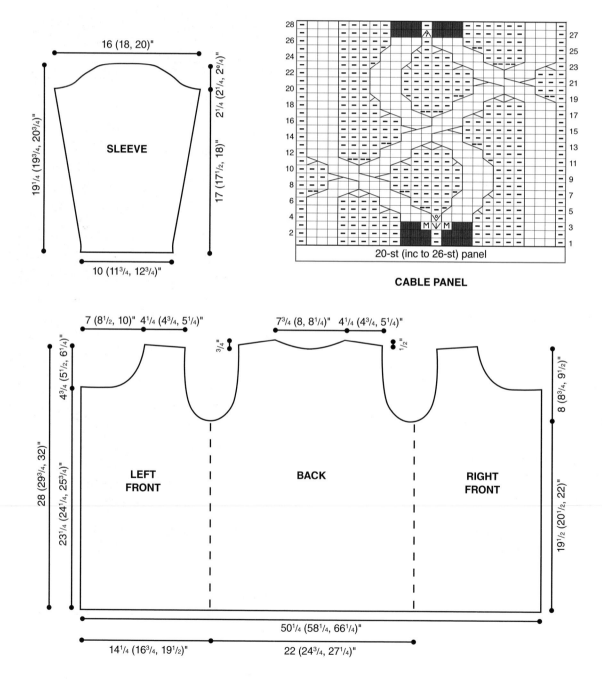

16 (18, 20)"

2¼ (2¼, 2⁶⁄₄)"

SLEEVE

19¼ (19¾, 20¾)"

17 (17½, 18)"

10 (11¾, 12¾)"

20-st (inc to 26-st) panel

CABLE PANEL

7 (8½, 10)"   4¼ (4¾, 5¼)"   7¾ (8, 8¼)"   4¼ (4¾, 5¼)"

4¾ (5½, 6¼)"

¾"   ½"

8 (8¾, 9½)"

28 (29¾, 32)"

LEFT FRONT   BACK   RIGHT FRONT

23¼ (24¼, 25¾)"

19½ (20½, 22)"

50¼ (58¼, 66¼)"

14¼ (16¾, 19½)"   22 (24¾, 27¼)"

Bobbles Beyond Compare

Work only one cable twist and one bobble every eighth row in a super bulky yarn for a quick, easy and very striking scarf to wrap up in. This is a great introductory project to cables and bobbles.

Design by Daniela Nii

Skill Level
■■■□ INTERMEDIATE

Finished Size
7½ x 68 inches

Materials
- Rowan Big Wool (super bulky weight; 100% merino wool; 87 yds/ 100g per skein): 4 skeins ice blue #021
- Size 15 (10mm) straight needles or size needed to obtain gauge
- Cable needle

Gauge
30 sts and 20 rnds (1 rep of Main Cable pat) = 7½ inches x 5 inches.

Exact gauge is not critical to this project.

Special Abbreviations
1 over 1 Right Cross (1/1 RC): Knit into 2nd st on LH needle, then knit into first st and slip both sts tog off LH needle.

4 over 4 Left Cross (4/4 LC): Sl 4 to cn and hold in front, k4, k4 from cn.

4 over 4 Right Cross (4/4 RC): Sl 4 to cn and hold in back, k4, k4 from cn.

Make Bobble (MB): [K1-tbl, yo, k1, yo, k1-tbl] all in same st (5 sts), turn; p5, turn; k5, turn; p5, turn; ssk, k1, slip first st over just-knit st, k2tog, pass both sts to LH needle and slip 2nd st over first st; slip back to RH needle—1 st rem.

Edge st: K1 at beg of row; sl 1 pwise wyif at end of row.

Pattern Stitch
Main Cable (30 sts)
Row 1 (RS): Edge st, p1, 1/1 RC, p3, k16, p3, 1/1 RC, p1, edge st.

Row 2 and all WS rows: Edge st, k1, p2, k3, p16, k3, p2, k1, edge st.
Row 3: Rep Row 1.
Row 5: Edge st, p1, 1/1 RC, p3, k3, MB, k4, 4/4 RC, p3, 1/1 RC, p1, edge st.
Rows 7, 9, 11 and 13: Rep Row 1.
Row 15: Edge st, p1, 1/1 RC, p3, 4/4 LC, k4, MB, k3, p3, 1/1 RC, p1, edge st.
Rows 17 and 19: Rep Row 1.
Row 20: Rep Row 2.
Rep Rows 1–20 for pat.

Special Technique

Felted Join: If using wool or other animal fiber, join 2 ends of yarn as follows: Fray ½ to 1 inch of both yarn ends, then moisten them. Overlap the frayed ends and place them between your palms. Briskly roll the yarn between your palms. The heat and friction will fuse (felt) the ends together. Continue knitting.

Pattern Notes

To join a new ball of yarn, use the Felted Join technique for a nearly invisible join.

A chart is included for those preferring to work Main Cable pattern from a chart. The chart shows right-side rows only. For wrong-side rows, maintain edge stitches and work all other stitches as they present themselves.

Scarf

Cast on 30 sts.

Ribbing

Rows 1 and 3 (WS): Edge st, k1, [p2, k2] 7 times, p2, k1, edge st.

Rows 2 and 4 (RS): Edge st, p1, [1/1 RC, p2] 7 times, 1/1 RC, p1, edge st.

Row 5: Rep Row 1.

Body

Work [Rows 1–20 of Main Cable pat] 13 times.

Ribbing

Rep Rows 2–5 of ribbing.

Bind off all sts kwise.

Finishing

Weave in all ends. Block as desired. ●

STITCH KEY
- + Edge st
- – K on RS, p on WS
- ☐ P on RS, k on WS
- ● MB
- ⧖ 1/1 RC
- 4/4 RC
- 4/4 LC

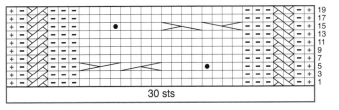

MAIN CABLE

Note: Chart shows RS rows only. Maintaining edge sts, work all sts on WS rows as they present themselves.

Drunken Cable Cowl

What would otherwise be a horseshoe cable is sent askew by working the left and right cable crossings on different rounds. Worked in a super bulky, thick-and-thin yarn, the cables become more and more abstract on this slouchy cowl.

Design by Amy Polcyn

. . . .

Skill Level
 EASY

Finished Measurements
Circumference: 33 inches
Length: 11 inches

Materials

- Aslan Trends Fashionist (super bulky weight; 78% acrylic/22% wool; 44 yds/100g per ball): 5 balls purple #138
- Size 15 (10mm) 24-inch circular needle or size needed to obtain gauge
- Cable needle

Gauge
12 sts and 8 rnds = 4 inches/10cm in Drunken Cable pat.

To save time, take time to check gauge.

Special Abbreviations
5 over 5 Right Cross (5/5 RC): Sl 5 to cn and hold in back, k5, k5 from cn.

5 over 5 Left Cross (5/5 LC): Sl 5 to cn and hold in front, k5, k5 from cn.

Make 1 (M1): Insert LH needle from front to back under the running thread between the last st worked and next st on LH needle; knit into the back of resulting loop.

Pattern Stitch
Drunken Cable (multiple of 20 sts)
Rnds 1 and 2: Knit around.
Rnd 3: *K10, 5/5 LC; rep from * around.
Rnd 4: Knit around.

Rnd 5: *5/5 RC, k10; rep from * around.
Rnds 6–10: Knit around.
Rep Rnds 1–10 for pat.

Cowl
Cast on 90 sts. Place marker and join, being careful not to twist the sts.

Rnds 1–3: *K5, p5; rep from * around.

Inc rnd: *K9, M1; rep from * around—100 sts.

Work in Drunken Cable pat until cowl measures approx 9 inches.

Dec rnd: *K8, k2tog; rep from * around—90 sts.

Next 3 rnds: Rep Rnds 1–3.

Bind off loosely in pat.

Finishing
Weave in ends. Block lightly. ●

STITCH KEY
☐ Knit
5/5 RC
5/5 LC

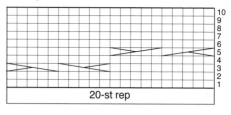

20-st rep

DRUNKEN CABLE

Simplicity Cowl

Enjoy the simple pleasures in life when you make this easy cabled cowl.

Design by Tabetha Hedrick

. . . .

Skill Level
■■□□ EASY

Finished Measurements
Circumference: 40 inches
Length: 20 inches

Materials
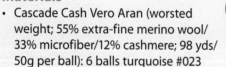
- Cascade Cash Vero Aran (worsted weight; 55% extra-fine merino wool/33% microfiber/12% cashmere; 98 yds/50g per ball): 6 balls turquoise #023
- Size 8 (5mm) needles or size needed to obtain gauge
- Cable needle

4 MEDIUM

Gauge
20 sts and 22 rows = 4 inches/10cm in Cable Rib pat (washed and blocked, moderately stretched).

To save time, take time to check gauge over blocked swatch.

Special Abbreviation
2 over 2 Left Cross (2/2 LC): Sl 2 to cn and hold in front, k2, k2 from cn.

Pattern Stitch
Cable Rib (multiple of 10 sts + 6)
Row 1 and all WS rows: Sl 1, k1, p2, k2, *p4, k2, p2, k2; rep from * to end.
Row 2 (RS): Sl 1, p1, k2, p2, *k4, p2, k2, p2; rep from * to end.
Row 3: Sl 1, k1, p2, k2, *p4, k2, p2, k2; rep from * to end.
Row 4: Sl 1, p1, k2, p2, *2/2 LC, p2, k2, p2; rep from * to end.
Row 6: Rep Row 2.
Rep Rows 1–6 for pat.

Pattern Note
Cowl is worked flat, and then seamed.

Cowl
Cast on 96 sts.

Set-up row (RS): P2, k2, p2, *k4, p2, k2, p2; rep from * to end.

Work Rows 1–6 of Cable Rib pat until piece measures approx 40 inches (blocked), ending with Row 2.

Bind off.

Finishing
Block piece to finished measurements.

Sew cast-on and bound-off edges together. ●

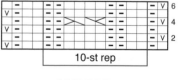

STITCH KEY
□ K on RS, p on WS
⊟ P on RS, k on WS
Ⅴ Sl 1
⧄⧅ 2/2 LC

CABLE RIB

10-st rep

Pebbles & Stones

Play it up with rich texture and depth with this easy cable-stitch pattern made in two different weights of yarn. When the cowl is worn wrapped twice around the neck, the "thick and thin" yarns intertwine around each other creating an intriguing look.

Design by Yumiko Alexander

. . . .

Skill Level
 EASY

Finished Measurements
Circumference: 80 inches
Length: 6 inches

Materials
- Cascade 128 Chunky (bulky weight; 100% Peruvian Highland wool; 128 yds/100g per skein): 2 skeins natural #8012 (A)
- Cascade Magnum (super bulky weight; 100% Peruvian Highland wool; 123 yds/250g per skein): 1 skein natural #8012 (B)
- Size 13 (9mm) needles or size needed to obtain gauge
- Size 19 (15mm) needles or size needed to obtain gauge
- Cable needle

Gauge
1 rep of Cable Panel (8 sts and 12 rows) = 2 inches wide x 3½ inches long with smaller needles and A (blocked).

1 rep of Cable Panel (8 sts and 12 rows) = 3 inches wide x 5 inches long with larger needles and B (blocked).

To save time, take time to check gauge.

Special Abbreviations
2 over 2 Left Purl Cross (2/2 LPC): Sl 2 to cn and hold in front, p2, k2 from cn.

2 over 2 Right Purl Cross (2/2 RPC): Sl 2 to cn and hold in back, k2, p2 from cn.

Make 1 (M1): Insert LH needle from front to back under the running thread between the last st worked and next st on LH needle; knit into the back of resulting loop.

Pattern Stitch
Cable Panel (8-st panel)
Rows 1, 3 and 5 (WS): P2, k4, p2.
Rows 2 and 4 (RS): K2, p4, k2.
Row 6: 2/2 LPC, 2/2 RPC.
Rows 7, 9 and 11: K2, p4, k2.
Rows 8 and 10: P2, k4, p2.
Row 12: 2/2 RPC, 2/2 LPC.
Rep Rows 1–12 for pat.

Pattern Note
Cowl is made by knitting 2 long rectangles, then joining them to form a ring.

Cowl

Rectangle 1
With smaller needles and A, cast on 20 sts.

Row 1 (RS): K1, [k1, M1, p4, M1, k1] 3 times, k1—26 sts.

Row 2: K1, work [Cable Panel Row 1] 3 times across, k1.

Maintaining first and last sts in St st, work in established pat until piece measures approx 40 inches, ending with Cable Panel Row 4.

Bind-off row (WS): Bind off while dec in pat as follows: P1, [p1, p2tog, k2, p2tog-tbl, p1] 3 times, p1.

Rectangle 2
With larger needles and B, cast on 12 sts.

Row 1 (RS): [K1, M1, p4, M1, k1] twice—16 sts.

Row 2 (WS): Work [Cable Panel Row 1] twice (there are no selvage sts).

Work even until piece measures approx 40 inches, ending with Cable Panel Row 4.

Bind-off row (WS): Bind off while dec in pat as follows: [p1, p2tog, k2, p2tog-tbl, p1] twice.

Finishing

Weave in all ends. Block pieces.

Using A, sew the cast-on edges of the 2 rectangles together, and then sew the bound-off edges together to form a ring. •

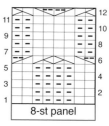

STITCH KEY

☐	K on RS, p on WS
–	P on RS, k on WS
⟋	2/2 LPC
⟍	2/2 RPC

8-st panel

CABLE PANEL

Talik

This ethnic-inspired, deeply textured scarf is quick and easy to knit, with a simple but stunning combination of XOXO cables and giant bobbles worked in a bulky earth-tone yarn.

Design by Ashley Forde Rao

Skill Level
■■□□ EASY

Finished Measurements
7 x 62 inches

Materials
- Brown Sheep Company Lamb's Pride Bulky (bulky weight; 85% wool/15% mohair; 125 yds/113g per skein): 3 skeins rust #M97
- Size 9 (5.5mm) needles or size needed to obtain gauge
- Cable needle

5 BULKY

Gauge
19 sts and 18 rows = 4 inches in Cable pat.

13 sts and 19 rows = 4 inches in St st.

To save time, take time to check gauge.

Special Abbreviations
2 over 2 Left Cross (2/2 LC): Sl 2 to cn and hold in front, k2, k2 from cn.

2 over 2 Right Cross (2/2 RC): Sl 2 to cn and hold in back, k2, k2 from cn.

Make Bobble (MB): *[K1, p1, k1] all in same st; rep from * once more, turn; p6, turn; k1, ssk, k2tog, k1, turn; p2tog twice, turn; k2.

Pattern Stitches
Rib (34 sts)
Row 1 (RS): Sl 1, [k2, p4] 5 times, k3.
Row 2: Sl 1, [p2, k4] 5 times, p3.
Rep Rows 1 and 2 for pat.

Cable (34 sts)
Row 1 and all WS rows: Sl 1, [p8, k4] twice, p9.
Row 2 (RS): Sl 1, [k8, p4] 2 times, k9.
Row 4: Sl 1, [2/2 LC, 2/2 RC, p4] twice, 2/2 LC, 2/2 RC, k1.
Row 6: Sl 1, [k8, p1, MB, p1] twice, k9.
Row 8: Sl 1, [2/2 RC, 2/2 LC, p4] twice, 2/2 RC, 2/2 LC, k1.
Row 10: Rep Row 2.
Row 12: Rep Row 8.
Row 14: Rep Row 2.
Row 16: Rep Row 4.
Rep Rows 1–16 for pat.

Pattern Note
Slip first stitch of all rows purlwise.

Scarf
Cast on 34 sts.

Edging
Set-up row (WS): P3, [k4, p2] 4 times, k4, p3.

Continue in Rib pat until piece measures 4 inches, ending with Row 1.

Body
Work Rows 1–16 of Cable pat until piece measures approx 58 inches, ending with Row 10 (RS).

Edging
Beg with Row 2, work Rib pat until piece measures 62 inches, ending with Row 1.

Bind off in rib on WS.

Finishing
Weave in all ends.

Lightly block to finished measurements. ●

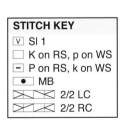

STITCH KEY
V	Sl 1
□	K on RS, p on WS
−	P on RS, k on WS
●	MB
⧓	2/2 LC
⧓	2/2 RC

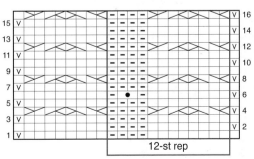

12-st rep

CABLE

General Information

Abbreviations & Symbols

[ ] work instructions within
brackets as many times
as directed

( ) work instructions within
parentheses in the place
directed

** repeat instructions following
the asterisks as directed

* repeat instructions following
the single asterisk as directed

" inch(es)

approx approximately
beg begin/begins/beginning
CC contrasting color
ch chain stitch
cm centimeter(s)
cn cable needle
dec decrease/decreases/
decreasing
dpn(s) double-point needle(s)
g gram(s)
inc increase/increases/increasing

k knit
k2tog knit 2 stitches together
kwise knitwise
LH left hand
m meter(s)
M1 make one stitch
MC main color
mm millimeter(s)
oz ounce(s)
p purl
pat(s) pattern(s)
p2tog purl 2 stitches together
psso pass slipped stitch over
pwise purlwise
rem remain/remains/remaining
rep repeat(s)
rev St st reverse stockinette stitch
RH right hand
rnd(s) rounds
RS right side
skp slip, knit, pass slipped stitch
over—1 stitch decreased

sk2p slip 1, knit 2 together,
pass slipped stitch over the
knit 2 together—2 stitches
decreased
sl slip
sl 1kwise slip 1 knitwise
sl 1pwise slip 1 purlwise
sl st slip stitch(es)
ssk slip, slip, knit these 2 stitches
together—a decrease
st(s) stitch(es)
St st stockinette stitch
tbl through back loop(s)
tog together
WS wrong side
wyib with yarn in back
wyif with yarn in front
yd(s) yard(s)
yfwd yarn forward
yo (yo's) yarn over(s)

Skill Levels

BEGINNER

Beginner projects
for first-time knitters
using basic stitches.
Minimal shaping.

EASY

Easy projects using
basic stitches, repetitive
stitch patterns, simple
color changes and
simple shaping
and finishing.

INTERMEDIATE

Intermediate projects
with a variety of stitches,
mid-level shaping
and finishing.

EXPERIENCED

Experienced projects
using advanced tech-
niques and stitches,
detailed shaping and
refined finishing.

Standard Yarn Weight System
Categories of yarn, gauge ranges, and recommended needle sizes

Yarn Weight Symbol & Category Names	0 LACE	1 SUPER FINE	2 FINE	3 LIGHT	4 MEDIUM	5 BULKY	6 SUPER BULKY
Type of Yarns in Category	Fingering 10-Count Crochet Thread	Sock, Fingering, Baby	Sport, Baby	DK, Light Worsted	Worsted, Afghan, Aran	Chunky, Craft, Rug	Super Chunky, Roving
Knit Gauge Range* in Stockinette Stitch to 4 inches	33–40 sts**	27–32 sts	23–26 sts	21–24 sts	16–20 sts	12–15 sts	6–11 sts
Recommended Needle in Metric Size Range	1.5–2.25mm	2.25–3.25mm	3.25–3.75mm	3.75–4.5mm	4.5–5.5mm	5.5–8mm	8mm and larger
Recommended Needle U.S. Size Range	000 to 1	1 to 3	3 to 5	5 to 7	7 to 9	9 to 11	11 and larger

* GUIDELINES ONLY: The above reflect the most commonly used gauges and needle sizes for specific yarn categories.

** Lace weight yarns are usually knitted on larger needles and hooks to create lacy, openwork patterns. Accordingly, a gauge range is difficult to determine. Always follow the gauge stated in your pattern.

Inches Into Millimeters & Centimeters
All measurements are rounded off slightly.

inches	mm	cm	inches	cm	inches	cm	inches	cm
⅛	3	0.3	5	12.5	21	53.5	38	96.5
¼	6	0.6	5½	14	22	56.0	39	99.0
⅜	10	1.0	6	15.0	23	58.5	40	101.5
½	13	1.3	7	18.0	24	61.0	41	104.0
⅝	15	1.5	8	20.5	25	63.5	42	106.5
¾	20	2.0	9	23.0	26	66.0	43	109.0
⅞	22	2.2	10	25.5	27	68.5	44	112.0
1	25	2.5	11	28.0	28	71.0	45	114.5
1¼	32	3.2	12	30.5	29	73.5	46	117.0
1½	38	3.8	13	33.0	30	76.0	47	119.5
1¾	45	4.5	14	35.5	31	79.0	48	122.0
2	50	5.0	15	38.0	32	81.5	49	124.5
2½	65	6.5	16	40.5	33	84.0	50	127.0
3	75	7.5	17	43.0	34	86.5		
3½	90	9.0	18	46.0	35	89.0		
4	100	10.0	19	48.5	36	91.5		
4½	115	11.5	20	51.0	37	94.0		

Knitting Basics

Increase (inc)

Two stitches in one stitch

Knit increase (kfb)

Knit the next stitch in the usual manner, but don't remove the stitch from the left needle. Place right needle behind left needle and knit again into the back of the same stitch. Slip original stitch off left needle.

Purl increase (pfb)

Purl the next stitch in the usual manner, but don't remove the stitch from the left needle. Place right needle behind left needle and purl again into the back of the same stitch. Slip original stitch off left needle.

Invisible Increase (M1)

There are several ways to make or increase one stitch.

Make 1 with Left Twist (M1L)

Insert left needle from front to back under the horizontal loop between the last stitch worked and next stitch on left needle.

   With right needle, knit into the back of this loop.

   To make this increase on the purl side, insert left needle in same manner and purl into the back of the loop.

Make 1 with Right Twist (M1R)

Insert left needle from back to front under the horizontal loop between the last stitch worked and next stitch on left needle.

   With right needle, knit into the front of this loop.

   To make this increase on the purl side, insert left needle in same manner and purl into the front of the loop.

Make 1 with Backward Loop over the right needle

With your thumb, make a loop over the right needle.

   Slip the loop from your thumb onto the needle and pull to tighten.

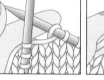

Make 1 in top of stitch below

Insert tip of right needle into the stitch on left needle one row below.

   Knit this stitch, then knit the stitch on the left needle.

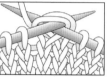

Decrease (dec)

Knit 2 together (k2tog)

Put tip of right needle through next two stitches on left needle as to knit. Knit these two stitches as one.

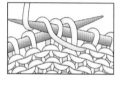

Purl 2 together (p2tog)

Put tip of right needle through next two stitches on left needle as to purl. Purl these two stitches as one.

Slip, Slip, Knit (ssk)

Slip next two stitches, one at a time, as to knit from left needle to right needle.

   Insert left needle in front of both stitches and knit them together.

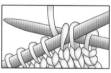

Slip, Slip, Purl (ssp)

Slip next two stitches, one at a time, as to knit from left needle to right needle. Slip these stitches back onto left needle keeping them twisted. Purl these two stitches together through back loops.

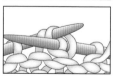

Kitchener Stitch

This method of weaving with two needles is used for the toes of socks and flat seams. To weave the edges together and form an unbroken line of stockinette stitch, divide all stitches evenly onto two knitting needles—one behind the other. Thread yarn into tapestry needle. Hold needles with wrong sides together and work from right to left as follows:

Step 1:
Insert tapestry needle into first stitch on front needle as to purl. Draw yarn through stitch, leaving stitch on knitting needle.

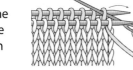

Step 1

Step 2:
Insert tapestry needle into the first stitch on the back needle as to purl. Draw yarn through stitch and slip stitch off knitting needle.

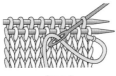

Step 2

Step 3:
Insert tapestry needle into the next stitch on same (back) needle as to knit, leaving stitch on knitting needle.

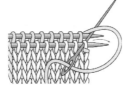

Step 3

Step 4:
Insert tapestry needle into the first stitch on the front needle as to knit. Draw yarn through stitch and slip stitch off knitting needle.

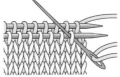

Step 4

Step 5:
Insert tapestry needle into the next stitch on same (front) needle as to purl. Draw yarn through stitch, leaving stitch on knitting needle.

Step 5

Repeat Steps 2 through 5 until one stitch is left on each needle. Then repeat Steps 2 and 4. Fasten off. Woven stitches should be the same size as adjacent knitted stitches.

Provisional Cast-On

The provisional cast-on has a variety of uses. It starts with a crochet chain on a crochet hook about the same size as the knitting needle. A chart is given below of crochet hooks that correspond most closely to knitting needle sizes.

Crochet Hook	Knitting Needle
E	4
F	5
G	6
H	8
I	9
J	10
K	10½

To work this type of cast-on, start with a crochet chain one or two stitches more than the number of stitches to be cast on for the pattern you are working. If the edge is to be decorative or removed to work in the opposite direction then the chain should be made with a contrasting color.

Once the chain is completed, with a knitting needle, pick up and knit in the back bar of each chain (Photo 1) until the required number of stitches is on the needle. Continue to work the pattern as given in the instructions.

Some instructions indicate that the provisional cast-on be removed so the piece can be worked in the opposite direction. In this case, hold the work with the cast-on edge at the top. Undo one loop of the crochet chain, inserting the knitting needle into the stitch below the chain. (This stitch is on the original first row of knitting.) Continue to undo the crochet chain until all the stitches are on the needle (Photo 2). This provides a row of stitches ready to work in the opposite direction.

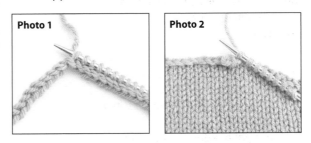

Photo 1 | Photo 2

HOUSE of WHITE BIRCHES PUBLISHERS SINCE 1947

Cable Ready is published by DRG, 306 East Parr Road, Berne, IN 46711. Printed in USA. Copyright © 2011 DRG. All rights reserved. This publication may not be reproduced in part or in whole without written permission from the publisher.

RETAIL STORES: If you would like to carry this pattern book or any other DRG publications, visit DRGwholesale.com.

Every effort has been made to ensure that the instructions in this pattern book are complete and accurate. We cannot, however, take responsibility for human error, typographical mistakes or variations in individual work. Please visit AnniesCustomerCare.com to check for pattern updates.

ISBN: 978-1-59217-338-9

1 2 3 4 5 6 7 8 9

Photo Gallery

6

9

13

24

19

31

34

36

38

41